*Commissioned to celebrate the bicentennial of First United Methodist Church, Lancaster, PA
and to celebrate the 300th anniversary of the birth of Charles Wesley;
presented by the Chancel Choir under the direction of Dr. Brian H. Norcross*

TESTAMENT OF
PRAISE

A CELEBRATION OF FAITH

Words by Charles Wesley
Music by Joseph M. Martin

Orchestrations by Brant Adams

4	Voices of Praise
19	Love Divine, All ' Excelling
29	Thankful for O
36	A Call to Serv
48	Jesus, Lover of My
57	And Can It Be?

Performance Time (if performed as a complete work): ca. 30 minutes

ISBN 9-781-5923-5157-2

SHAWNEE ✦ PRESS

EXCLUSIVELY DISTRIBUTED BY

HAL•LEONARD®

7777 W. BLUEMOUND RD. P.O. BOX 13819 MILWAUKEE, WI 53213

In Australia Contact:
Hal Leonard Australia Pty. Ltd.
4 Lentara Court
Cheltenham, Victoria, 3192 Australia
Email: ausadmin@halleonard.com.au

Visit Hal Leonard Online at
www.halleonard.com

Visit Shawnee Press Online at
www.shawneepress.com

FOREWORD

When we consider the music of our faith, the anthems and hymns whose inspiring texts are so much a part of our shared language of worship, we stand amazed by the treasures we find. Each generation contributes great composers, lyricists and poets who lift up their crafts in sacred purpose. This legacy of praise is an important element of what it is to be part of the universal church.

This present work celebrates the words and message of Charles Wesley (1707-1788). The work of this devout writer has become part of our common Christian vocabulary, transcending the differences of denomination and dogma. We are community when we celebrate worship with the words of Wesley for they are words filled with deep emotion and thoughtful theology. They represent some of the most insightful expressions in all of Christian hymnody.

The six texts chosen for this collection represent a few of the most important concepts found in Wesley's oeuvre. The messages of Worship, Love, Thanksgiving, Service, Life and Grace are foundational to our Christian journey and they are subjects that permeate Wesley's work. Many of these texts remain standards in denominational hymnals to this day.

May these beloved words and the truth they proclaim resonate once again as they are raised in these anthems. As you study and present this work may your song echo in the hearts of your church and may your lives become a "Testament of Praise."

JOSEPH M. MARTIN

PERFORMANCE NOTES

This book may be used as a collection of individual anthems or presented as a longer multi-movement work. In the back of this book you will find a sample service plan along with suggested litanies, congregation hymn singing, narration and possible use of banners. Most of the words in this sample are adapted from scripture or the words of Wesley himself.

Please feel free to make this presentation your own by adding to or eliminating elements that are not appropriate for your individual church. This outline is only one possible realization of a worship event planned around these beloved expressions of faith.

Voices of Praise

"Praise the Lord Who Reigns Above," "Sing with Glad Anticipation,"
"Rejoice, the Lord is King," "O for a Thousand Tongues to Sing,"

Words by
CHARLES WESLEY (1707-1788)

Arranged by
JOSEPH M. MARTIN (BMI)

* Tune: AMSTERDAM, James Nares (1715-1783)

all His great-ness show. Praise Him for His

no - ble__ deeds. Praise Him__ for His match - less__ power.__

Him, from whom all good pro - ceeds,__ let all things__ praise the

8

* Tune: REGENT SQUARE, Henry T. Smart (1813-1879)

A858

full sal - va - tion. Je - sus doth His glo - ry bring. Hal - le - lu - jah, hal - le - lu - jah! God om - nip - o - tent is King.

Tune: DARWALL'S 148TH, John Darwall (1731-1789)

8581

say, re - joice! Lift up your

heart! Lift up your voice! Re -

joice, a - gain I say, re -

joice!

111

SOPRANO DESCANT

Congregation may sing melody *

Al - le -

** O   for   a   thou - sand

lu - ia,   al - le - lu - ia,   al - le - lu - ia.

tongues to sing   my   great Re - deem - er's   praise.   The

*   Part for Congregation may be found on page 71.
** Tune: AZMON, Carl G. Gläser (1784-1829)

A8581

Al - le - lu - ia, the tri - umphs of His

glo - ries of my God and King, the___ tri - umphs of His

grace. My

grace. My

God_____ as - sist me to pro -

gra-cious Mas - ter and my God, as - sist me to pro -

claim, to spread thro' all the earth a-broad the

claim, to spread thro' all the earth a-broad__ the__

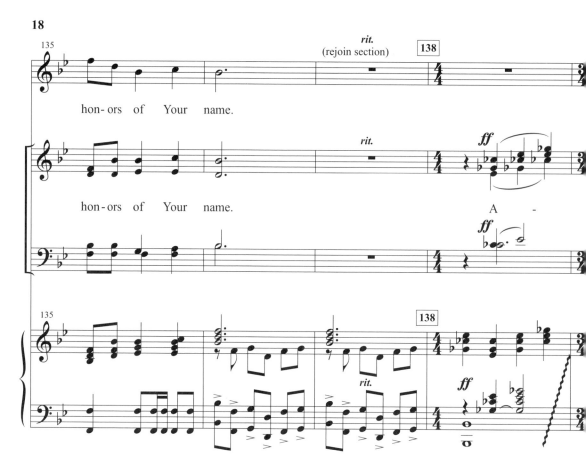

hon- ors of Your name.

hon- ors of Your name. A -

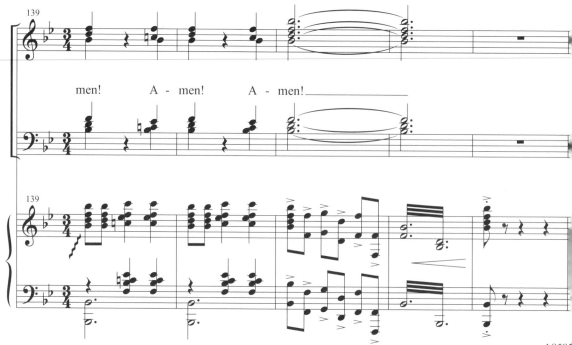

men! A - men! A - men!

Love Divine, All Loves Excelling

Tune: BUNESSAN
Gaelic Melody
Arranged by
JOSEPH M. MARTIN (BMI)

Words by
CHARLES WESLEY (1707-1788)

to earth___ come down;___

fix___ in us Thy hum - ble dwell -

ing. All___ Thy faith - ful mer - cies

crown.___

heart.

Fin - ish then, Thy new cre -

a - tion. Pure and spot -

24

less let_____ us be._____

Let_____ us see Thy great_____ sal -

va - tion per - fect - ly

re - stored___ in Thee._____

Changed___ from glo - ry in - to

glo - ry, till in heav'n we take our place.

Till we cast our crowns be -

vine,

Love di - vine.

Thankful for Our Every Blessing

Words by
CHARLES WESLEY (1707-1788)

Music by
JOSEPH M. MARTIN (BMI)

30

A8581

He dis - pels our sin and sad - ness,

life im - parts,

cheers our hearts,

34

Us He leads to a feast in feeds. Leads us to a feast in heav - en, to a feast in heav - en, to a feast in

A8581

A Call to Service

"A Charge to Keep I Have" and "The Vigilance Our Lord Demands"

Words by
CHARLES WESLEY (1707-1788)

Music by
JOSEPH M. MARTIN (BMI)

A8581

have,   a God to glo - ri - fy,   a

nev - er dy - ing soul to save, and   fit it for the

sky.___   To serve the pres - ent

To__ watch__ and__ pray, and

Help me to watch and pray, and

on Thy - self re - ly,

on Thy - self, Thy - self__ re - ly,

as - sured, if I my trust be - tray, I

our ac - tive zeal,_____

pa - tient toil,_____

_____ our ut - most strife to do_____ His_____

will._____

By faith and pen - i -

A8581

God to glo - ri - fy, a nev - er dy - ing

soul to save, and fit it for the sky.____

To serve the pres - ent age, my

commissioned by the Choir of St. Armands Key Lutheran Church in Sarasota, FL
as a loving tribute to our dearest friend, Vern Lautner,
and his lifelong devotion to praising his Lord with song

Jesus, Lover of My Soul

Words by
CHARLES WESLEY (1707-1788)

Music by
JOSEPH M. MARTIN (BMI

* Alternate words by Joseph M. Martin.

A8581

50

A8581

com - fort __ me. _____

All my trust on Thee is stayed, all my help from

Thee I bring. Cov - er my de - fense - less head with the

sha - dow   of   Thy___ wing,_____   with   the   shad - ow

of_____ Thy_____ wing.

allargando

Plen-teous grace with Thee is found, grace to cov - er all my sin._____ Let the heal - ing streams a - bound, make and keep me pure with - in._____

And Can It Be?

Tune: SAGINA
by THOMAS CAMPBELL (1777-1844)
Arranged by
JOSEPH M. MARTIN (BMI)

Words by
CHARLES WESLEY (1707-1788)

With great power (♩ = ca. 128)

And can it be that

A8581

58

I____ should____ gain an in - t'rest____ in the____ Sav - ior's____ blood?

Died He for me, who____ caused His

A858

God,____ should____ die____ for____ me?

He left His

Fa - ther's throne____ a - bove._____ So free,____ so____

help - less race!

'Tis____ mer - cy

all im - mense____ and____ free,____ for

64

A858

God,___ should___ die for me?

allargando

With triumphant jubilation (♩ = ca. 116-120)

No con - dem - na - tion now___ I___

With triumphant jubilation (♩ = ca. 116-120)

clothed___ in righ - teous - ness di - vine. Bold,___ I ap - proach th'e - ter - nal___ throne,___ and

God,___ should___ die for

me? A - le - lu - ia! Sing al - le -

lu - ia! Al - le - lu - ia! Sing al - le -

A - le - lu - ia! Sing!

The publisher hereby grants permission to reprint the material included in the box below for the purpose of congregational participation. Copies must include all information within the box below; i.e., title, all credits and copyright notice.

Voices of Praise

"O for a Thousand Tongues to Sing"

Tune: AZMON
by CARL G. GLÄSER, 1784-1829
Arranged by
JOSEPH M. MARTIN (BMI)

Words by
CHARLES WESLEY (1707-1788)

CONGREGATION *(in unison)*

O for a thou - sand tongues to sing my great Re - deem - er's praise. The glo - ries of my God and King, the tri - umphs of His grace.

My gra - cious Mas - ter and my God, as - sist me to pro - claim, to spread thro' all the earth a - broad the hon - ors of Your name.

Reproduced by Permission of the Publisher

The publisher hereby grants permission to reprint the material included in the box below for the purpose of congregational participation. Copies must include all information within the box below; i.e., title, all credits and copyright notice.

LITANY

Leader: Praise ye the Lord. Praise God in his sanctuary.
Praise him in the firmament of his power.

People: Good and right it is to sing,*
In every time and place,
Glory to our heavenly King,
The God of truth and grace.

Leader: O come let us sing to the Lord.
Let us make a joyful noise to the Rock of our salvation.

People: All praise to our Redeeming Lord!

Leader: Let us come before his presence with thanksgiving.

People: All thanks be to God!

Leader: O come, let us worship and bow down.
Let us kneel before the Lord our Maker.

People: Then let us adore and give him his right:
all glory and power, all wisdom and might.

Leader: For the Lord is a great God, and a great King above all

People: gods.

Leader: Rejoice the Lord is King! All praise to God above!

People: Lift up your hearts!

Leader: Hallelujah!

People: Lift up your voice!

Leader: Glory be to God on high!

People: Praise the Lord, ye saints and sing; all the powers of music bring.

Hallelujah! This is our testament of praise!

Sources from Charles Wesley (1707-1788) and the Bible
* The original text read "Meet and right it is to sing,"

anner 1: "Worship" *(This and subsequent banners may be brought in and placed in an appropriate location during the introduction of the anthem that follows.)*

"Voices of Praise"
(Anthem 1)

Worship Leader: Come, and let us sweetly join
Christ to praise in hymns divine!
Give we all, with one accord,
Glory to our common Lord.

Congregational Hymn: "Ye Servants of God" (Charles Wesley)
Recommended tunes: LYONS or HANOVER

Prayer: *(Pastor or Worship Leader)*

eader 1: In this was manifested the love of God toward us, because that God sent His only begotten Son into the world, that we might live through Him.

eader 2: Beloved, if God so loved us, we also ought to love one another.

anner 2: "Love"

"Love Divine, All Loves Excelling"
(Anthem 2)

Congregational Hymn: "O For a Heart to Praise My God" (Charles Wesley)
Recommended tunes: MAITLAND, ST.ANNE or WINCHESTER OLD

eader 1: Give thanks to the Lord, for He is good.
His mercy endures forever.

Reader 2: It is a good thing to give thanks unto God and to sing praise unto His name. O Lord, how great are Your works!

Banner 3: "Thanksgiving"

"Thankful for Our Every Blessing"
(Anthem 3)

Reader 1:   As we have therefore opportunity, let us do good unto a people. And whatsoever you do, do it heartily, as to the Lord…

Reader 2:   Live a life worthy of the Lord:
      bearing good fruit in every good work,
      growing in knowledge of God,
      being strengthened with all power according to H glorious might.

Banner 4:   "Service"

"A Call to Service"
(Anthem 4)

Congregational Hymn: Soldiers of Christ, Arise" (Charles Wesley)
Recommended tune: DIADEMATA

Reader 1:   "I am the resurrection, and the life: he that believeth in me, though he were dead, yet shall he live."

Reader 2:   These things have I written unto you that believe on the name of the Son of God; that ye may know that ye have eternal life, and that ye may believe on the name of the Son of God.

Choir and Congregation: For God so loved the world that He gave his only begotten Son, that whoever believes in Him should not perish but have eternal life.

Banner 5:   "Life"

"Jesus, Lover of My Soul"
(Anthem 5)

Reader 1:   God commendeth His love toward us, in that while we were yet sinners, Christ died for us.

Reader 2:   Where sin abounded, grace did much more abound.

eader 1:   Not by works of righteousness which we have done, but according to His mercy He saved us, by the washing of regeneration, and renewing of the Holy Spirit: which He shed on us abundantly through Jesus Christ our Savior:

eader 2:   That being justified by His grace, we should be made heirs according to the hope of eternal life.

anner 6:   "Grace"

"And Can It Be?"
(Anthem 6)

inal Blessing: …and now may you go from this place and take with you
(Worship Leader)   this word of encouragement, that your life might be a testament of praise.

May the heart of your faith be reflected in your daily *worship* and in the *love* you share with others. May your spirit be filled with a song of *thanksgiving* and as you celebrate God's blessing may you be challenged to a deeper commitment to *service*. May you live your days in hope delighting in God's promises of abundant and eternal *life*… And may the music of your life be a neverending song of *grace*. Go in peace. Amen!